Growing with Technology

T0200366

Level 1

Gary B. Shelly
Thomas J. Cashman
Rachel Biheller Bunin

COURSE TECHNOLOGY
CENGAGE Learning™

Australia • Brazil • Japan • Korea • Mexico • Singapore • Spain • United Kingdom • United States

COURSE TECHNOLOGY
CENGAGE Learning™

Growing with Technology, Level 1
Gary B. Shelly
Thomas J. Cashman
Rachel Biheller Bunin

Managing Editor: Cheryl Ouellette

Marketing Manager: Katie McAllister

Senior Product Manager: Alexandra Arnold

Product Manager: Erin Runyon

Associate Product Manager: Reed Cotter

Editorial Assistant: Emilie Perreault

Print Buyer: Denise Powers

Director of Production: Becky Herrington

Production Manager: Doug Cowley

Copy Editor: Lyn Markowicz

Proofreader: Kim Kosmatka

Illustrators: Stephanie Nance, Andrew Bartel, Becky Herrington, Betty Hopkins

Cover Design: Becky Herrington, Ken Russo

Interior Design: Betty Hopkins, Becky Herrington

Photo Research: Betty Hopkins

Compositors: Betty Hopkins, Jeanne Black

© 2003 Course Technology, Cengage Learning

For product information and technology assistance, contact us at
Cengage Learning Customer & Sales Support, 1-800-354-9706

For permission to use material from this text or product, submit all requests online at **cengage.com/permissions**
Further permissions questions can be emailed to
permissionrequest@cengage.com

ISBN-10: 0-7895-6843-8

ISBN-13: 978-0-7895-6843-4

Course Technology
25 Thomson Place
Boston, Massachusetts 02210
USA

Cengage Learning is a leading provider of customized learning solutions with office locations around the globe, including Singapore, the United Kingdom, Australia, Mexico, Brazil, and Japan. Locate your local office at:
international.cengage.com/region

Cengage Learning products are represented in Canada by Nelson Education, Ltd.

For your lifelong learning solutions, visit **course.cengage.com**

Purchase any of our products at your local college store or at our preferred online store **www.ichapters.com**

PHOTO CREDITS:
Page 1 Students with Teacher, Copyright © BananaStock/BananaStock, Ltd./PictureQuest LLC 1998-2003. All rights reserved; *Page 3* Dell Computer GX150MT, Courtesy of Dell Computer Corp., Photographer Carrington Weems; *Page 4* Mouse, Courtesy of ACCO Brand and Kensington Corp.; *Page 4* Mouse, Copyright © 2003 Microsoft Corporation. All rights reserved; *Page 4* Mouse Red, Courtesy of Logitech, Inc.; *Page 21* Three children, Copyright © Stockbyte; *Page 27* Keyboarding, Copyright © 2002 AP Photo Archive. All rights reserved; *Page 28* Keyboarding, Copyright © BananaStock/BananaStock, Ltd./PictureQuest LLC 1998-2003. All rights reserved; *Page 47* Boy, Copyright © PictureQuest LLC 1998-2003. All rights reserved; *Page 51* Keyboard, Courtesy of ACCO Brand and Kensington Corp.; *Page 57* Boy with Laptop, Copyright © Stockbyte; *Page 119* Computer Class, Copyright © Stockbyte; All clipart, Copyright © www.clipart.com.

Printed in the United Kingdom by Ashford Colour Press

Print Number 08 Print Year 2018

Growing with Technology

Level 1

Contents

Chapter 1

Computer Foundations

Chapter 2

Getting Started with Keyboarding

Chapter 3

Creating Documents with a Word Processor

Chapter 4

Networks and the Internet

Chapter 5

Creating Graphics

Working with Presentation Software

Chapter 7

Working with Spreadsheets

	Pets	
1		
2	Type of Pet	Number
3	birds	3
4	cats	5
5	dogs	9
6	fish	4
7	other pets	2
8	Total	23

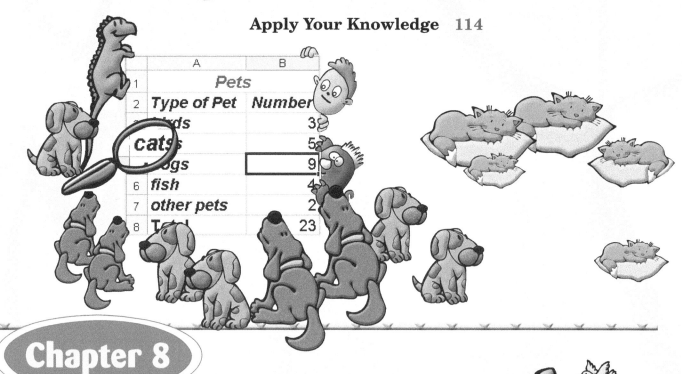

Chapter 8

Working with Information in Databases

Preface

The Shelly Cashman Series® offers the finest textbooks in computer education. We are proud of the fact that our textbook series has been the most widely used series in educational instruction and pleased to announce the addition of the *Growing with Technology* textbooks. The need for elementary teachers to teach essential technology skills to their students is our reason for the creation of the *Growing with Technology* series. These books continue with the innovation, quality, and reliability that you have come to expect from the Shelly Cashman Series.

The Shelly Cashman Series has been a leader in educational publishing for more than 30 years. This experience has allowed us to develop the perfect technology education program that starts students with the basics and gradually builds their skill sets. Through interesting lessons, activities, and projects, the *Growing with Technology* series is able to present elementary-aged students with core computing concepts and applications essential for future success while having fun! Students will follow the adventures of the book's cast of characters as they discover the skills needed to succeed with technology. The following characters identify the level of study:

Katie	Burton	Booker	Carmen	Dwayne	Yasmin
Level K	Level 1	Level 2	Level 3	Level 4	Level 5

Overview

Growing with Technology introduces elementary-aged students to the basics of computers and computer applications. The lessons in each book are organized into eight chapters that cover:

- Computer Foundations
- Keyboarding
- Word Processing
- Networks and the Internet
- Creating Graphics
- Presentation Graphics
- Spreadsheets
- Databases

Organization of the Textbooks

The *Growing with Technology* textbooks are organized so that the material is presented first with a chapter overview, followed by lessons, and concluding with an end-of-chapter activity. This book can be used for students in the K-2 level and can be read along with the students as they complete the lessons. We also have a *Big Book* version of our textbook available for shared reading. Through the colorful illustrations, diagrams, and succinct step-by-step activities, it is easy to work with the students through the lessons. Our textbook creates a successful learning environment for students to retain information.

Visually Stimulating Presentation

The book's cast of characters visually engages young learners while introducing valuable technology skills. Students will follow one character's journey through each level, making it fun for them to learn the concepts presented. A helper character, Red, provides insight, positive reinforcement, and assistance in the form of margin notes throughout the series.

> **Burton accompanies students through each lesson.**

Lessons and Activities   Student lessons combine basic computer and technology concepts with hands-on, step-by-step activities. Students are introduced to basic computer literacy concepts while acquiring common information and integration as well as problem-solving skills. They learn technology terminology appropriate for each task. The textbooks are designed so students can work through each lesson independently or in groups. *Growing with Technology* can be used in a variety of classroom settings:

- **Lab Setting**   A classroom with a one-to-one correlation between students and computers.

- **Classroom with Shared Computers**   A standard classroom with small groups of students required to share a computer. Students rotate using the computer to complete the lesson.

- **Classrooms with Teacher Aides**   A classroom with a teacher as well as a teacher aide. The teacher aide can instruct one or more students at a time.

Companion Web Site   A robust Web site provides interactivity through games and reinforcement tutorials (http://growing.course.com). The student Web site provides students with an opportunity to reinforce skills by using additional activities, games, flash cards, a glossary, and practice quizzes.

   The teacher Web site contains the following content:

- **Assessment Rubrics**   Determine the skills level of students.

- **Curriculum**   Integration activities provide examples of how to integrate computer skills across the curriculum.

- **Correlation Grids**   Map to common technology standards.

- **Data Files**   All the files necessary to work through each lesson.

- **Solution Files**   Solutions to all assignments.

- **Teacher Resource Materials**   The materials provided on our Teacher Resources CD-ROM will be provided on the teacher Web site in downloadable versions.

Reinforcement and Assessment   Well-structured student activities can make the difference between students merely participating in a class and students retaining the information they learn. Apply Your Knowledge activities at the end of each lesson reinforce what was learned through group and lesson exercises, while assessment rubrics quickly assess students' current level and progress.

Technology Generic   The technology presented is platform independent and software and version generic, so the books easily can be adapted to any classroom environment. Our teacher materials address the differences in the software and hardware as a way to help teachers. Here is a list of the more common software used for the lessons taught in these textbooks:

- **Microsoft Office**   Available for purchase through Microsoft (www.microsoft.com).

- **Microsoft Works**   Available for purchase through Microsoft (www.microsoft.com).

- **StarOffice**   Available for purchase through Sun Microsystems (www.sun.com).

- **AppleWorks**   Available for purchase through Apple Computer, Inc. (www.apple.com/appleworks).

Shelly Cashman Series Teacher Resources

Comprehensive teacher materials will help minimize time spent on class preparation and organization. The contents of the Teacher Resources CD-ROM are listed on the next page.

For each lesson, we provide the following:

- **Prepare** Any teacher knows that preparing for a lesson is a lot of work; therefore, we provide detailed information on how to prepare for each lesson.

- **Software** A list of all software and data files used in the lesson.

- **Using the Software** Information for teachers on how to use the software in the lesson to get the same results as the book examples.

- **Troubleshooting Tips** Helpful tips to avoid possible frustrations in the classroom, whether with the software or with the lesson structure.

- **Lesson Plan** Instructions on how to direct students through each lesson.

- **Additional Activities and Exercises** Creative suggestions for additional practice of skills learned in each lesson. We provide cross-curriculum activities, so students learn how to apply basic computer skills to many areas of their education and computer experience.

- **Using the Web Site** Instructions on how to use and integrate the Web site content effectively in the classroom.

- **End of Lesson** Solutions to each lesson, where applicable.

- **Assessment** Suggested assessment ideas to determine whether a student has successfully mastered the skills taught in the lesson.

The ancillaries that accompany these textbooks are a Teacher Resources CD-ROM (ISBN 0-619-20006-5) and *Big Books* for shared reading for kindergarten and first grade classrooms (Level K ISBN 0-619-20008-1 and Level 1 ISBN 0-619-20009-X). These ancillaries are available to adopters through your Course Technology representative or by calling the following telephone number: Primary, Middle, and High Schools, 1-800-824-5179.

Acknowledgments

The Shelly Cashman Series would not be the leading computer education series without the contributions of outstanding publishing professionals. First, and foremost, among them is Becky Herrington, director of production, designer, and illustrator. She is the heart and soul of the Shelly Cashman Series, and it is only through her leadership, dedication, and tireless efforts that superior products are made possible. Under Becky's direction, the following individuals made significant contributions to these books: Doug Cowley, production manager; Betty Hopkins, interior designer; Ken Russo, cover designer; Ginny Harvey, series specialist; Betty Hopkins and Jeanne Black, QuarkXPress compositors; Stephanie Nance, Andrew Bartel, and Betty Hopkins, illustrators; Lyn Markowicz; copy editor; Kim Kosmatka, proofreader; and Betty Hopkins, photo researcher.

Finally, we would like to thank Kristen Duerr, senior vice president and publisher; Chris Elkhill, senior vice president of the school market group; Cheryl Ouellette, managing editor; Chris Katsaropoulos, managing editor; Jim Quasney, series consulting editor; Alexandra Arnold, senior product manager; Erin Runyon, product manager; Reed Cotter, associate product manager; Jodi Dreissig, associate product manager; Emilie Perreault, editorial assistant; Marc Ouellette, online product manager; Cathlin McCullough, information architect; Peter Themistocles, senior online product manager; and Katie McAllister, marketing manager.

Gary B. Shelly

Thomas J. Cashman

Rachel Biheller Bunin

Chapter 1

Computer Foundations

People use computers for different tasks. Computers are in schools, at work, in stores, in banks, and in homes. Students use computers to write, to learn, and to play games. Computers help people count money and create art. You can use a computer, too!

What You Will Learn

In this chapter, you will learn about the different parts of a computer, the programs on a computer, and some rules to follow when you use a computer.

What Is a Computer?

A computer is a machine. It can help you learn and play games. It can help you work with numbers. You can use a computer to write letters or stories. Computers work with data. Input is the data you enter into a computer. Data is words, numbers, pictures, or sounds. A computer uses memory to store data. A computer processes the data. Output is what the computer produces. Output is information. Output can be words, numbers, pictures, or sounds.

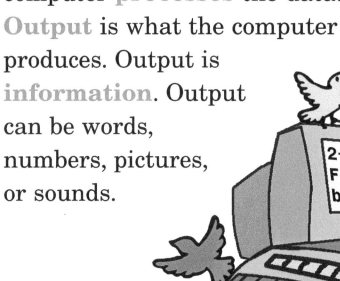

2+3=5
Five
birds

Parts of a Computer

The parts of the computer you can see and touch are called hardware. Another name for hardware is devices. You use an input device to enter data into the computer. The mouse and the keyboard are input devices.

The system unit has hardware inside it that processes the data. You use an output device to get information out of the computer. Information can be the answer, a picture, or a letter to your friend. Monitors, printers, and speakers are output devices.

A monitor shows you information on a screen like a television set. A printer prints the information on paper. A speaker lets you hear information.

monitor

system unit

printer

speaker

mouse

keyboard

Using a Mouse

The mouse is a pointing device. You move the mouse on your desk to move a pointer on the screen. You click the mouse button when the pointer is pointing to what you want. Clicking sends the message to the computer so the computer knows what you want. In this lesson, you will learn how to drag, point, click, and double-click the mouse to give commands to the computer.

Keep the mouse on top of the desk next to your computer. You put a mouse pad under a mouse. If you pick up the mouse, the pointer will not move when you move the mouse.

Pointers appear as different shapes. A pointer can be a line, an arrow, or a hand pointer. You will learn why pointers change shapes later.

When you want something, you can point to it.

To Use the Mouse

Steps

Be at your computer and it must be on.

1. To do these steps, your computer must be turned on and set up for you. Keep the mouse on the mouse pad. When you move the mouse on the mouse pad, the pointer on the screen moves to match how you move the mouse on the mouse pad.

2. Move the mouse toward you over the mouse pad. See the mouse pointer move down. Move the mouse away from you over the mouse pad. See the mouse pointer move up. Move the mouse to the side and back again. Move the mouse fast, and the mouse pointer moves fast.

3. The small pictures or images on your screen are called icons. Icons can be different sizes. The picture helps you know what will happen when you click the icon. Move the mouse to point to an icon.

4. You double-click to tell the computer you want that command. A mouse can have one or two buttons. To click, place your right hand on the mouse, put your pointer finger on the left mouse button — or on the one mouse button. Press the button quickly and then lift your finger up. That is a click.

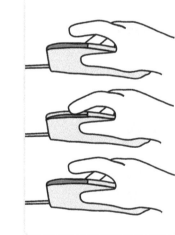

Did you hear the click sound?

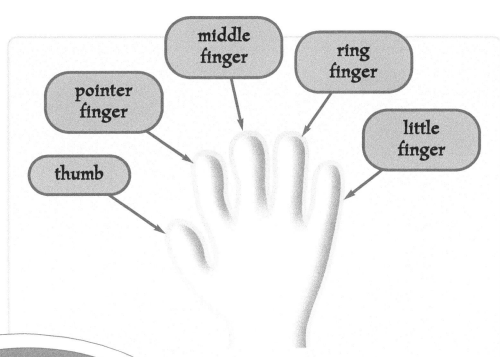

pointer finger

middle finger

ring finger

little finger

thumb

Practice double-clicking by tapping your fingers on your desk in a tap-tap — stop — tap-tap — stop pattern.

5. Sometimes you have to click two times to tell the computer what to do. **Double-click** means two very fast clicks. To double-click, you press the left mouse button two times — click click.

6. Sometimes you move the mouse to drag objects on the screen. An icon is one type of object. Point to an icon, press the left mouse button and hold the button down. Move the mouse to drag or pull the icon across the screen and then lift your finger from the mouse button. You dragged the icon to a new place.

left button

right button

Your mouse may have only one button.

Exploring the Keyboard

You use a keyboard to type letters, numbers, and symbols into the computer. A keyboard has letter, number, and symbol keys. The keys on the computer are not in ABC order. Some keys have letters and symbols. A $ is a symbol for money. A keyboard also has special keys that work with other keys. In this lesson, you will find keys on the keyboard.

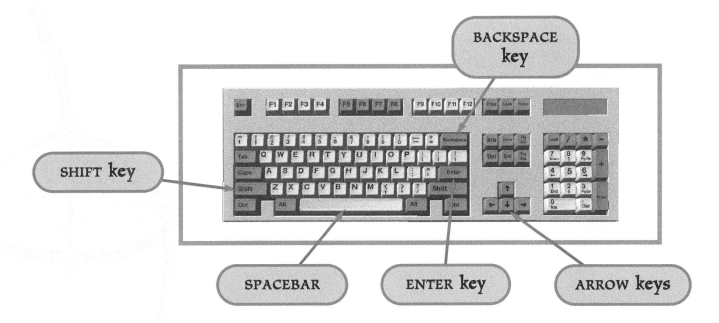

BACKSPACE key

SHIFT key

SPACEBAR

ENTER key

ARROW keys

To Explore the Keyboard

1. Look for the letter A on the keyboard. Press A.

2. Look for the letter B on the keyboard. Press B.

3. Find the SHIFT key. Press Shift. The SHIFT key is a special key. It works with other keys.

4. The SPACEBAR is a long bar at the bottom of the keyboard that looks like this [   ]. Press [   ].

5. Find the four ARROW keys. Press ↑ one time. Press ↓.

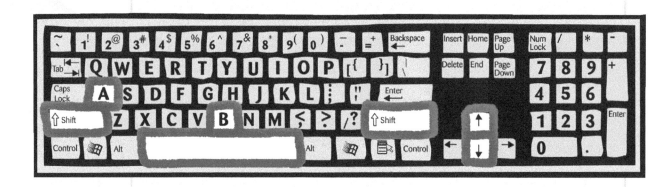

Computer Software

Computers work because of hardware and software. Software, also called a program, has the instructions that tell the computer what to do. You can touch hardware. You *cannot* touch software. Many different types of software are available. Games on a computer are software. Software can display or play sound, movies, and pictures. Word processors, paint programs, spreadsheets, and databases are the software you are going to learn about.

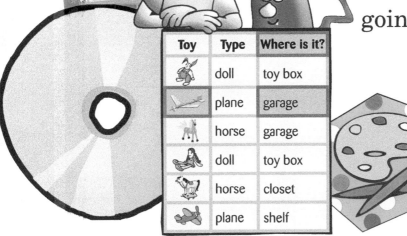

Toy	Type	Where is it?
	doll	toy box
	plane	garage
	horse	garage
	doll	toy box
	horse	closet
	plane	shelf

Using a CD-ROM

A CD-ROM is a flat round disk. To say the word CD-ROM, you say "sea dee rom." Sometimes CD-ROMs are called just CDs. CD stands for compact disc.

A CD-ROM stores software or data. A computer has a CD-ROM drive. The CD-ROM drive is the hardware that the computer uses to read what is on the CD-ROM.

Steps

To Use a CD-ROM

1. **Look at the CD-ROM. It has a very shiny side and a label side with a picture or words. Hold the CD by the edges with the label side up.**

2. Find the CD-ROM drive on the computer. Press the button to open the drive. Some CD-ROM drives are just slots on the front of the computer.

3. Very gently, put the CD-ROM in the drive with the label side up. Make sure the CD-ROM is laying flat. Press the button to close the drive.

4. Press the button to open the drive. When the drive opens, remove the CD-ROM.

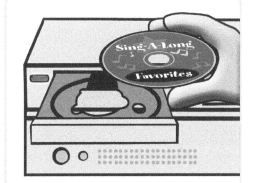

Computers can play music CDs.

Starting and Quitting a Program

Software also is called computer programs. Different types of programs are stored in your computer. To use a program, you have to start it. You start a program by using a command. The command might be an icon or a word on a menu. A menu is a list of commands. When you are done using the program, you quit or exit a program.

Steps

To Start and Quit a Program

1. When you turn on a computer, you will see icons on the screen. The space you see on the screen is called the desktop.

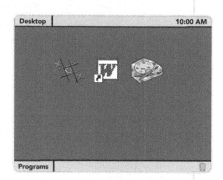

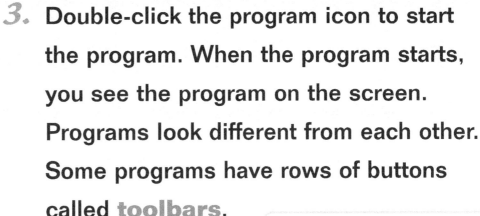

2. Use the mouse to point to a program icon on the desktop.

3. Double-click the program icon to start the program. When the program starts, you see the program on the screen. Programs look different from each other. Some programs have rows of buttons called **toolbars**.

The buttons have pictures on them to help you remember what each button does.

When you quit or exit a program, it still is stored in your computer.

4. Click the Close button to quit the program. When you close a program, the program is not running anymore.

Opening and Closing a File

Computers store data in files. A file stores words, pictures, or numbers. Software uses files. You save your work as a file. You open a file to work on it. You close a file when you are done. Just like you have a name, each file has a name. In this lesson, you first will open a file and then close it.

Steps

To Open and Close a File

1. Double-click the My Birthday File icon on the desktop. The name of this file is My Birthday File. The file opens. It is a birthday message. The screen shows the words and pictures that are in the file.

Desktop   10:00 AM

My Birthday File

Programs

2. **Click the Close button to close the file. You see the desktop on the screen again. The file still is stored in the computer, even though you cannot see it on the screen.**

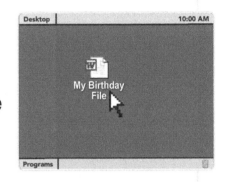

Using a Floppy Disk

When you use a computer, you can save your work in a file on a floppy disk. When you save a file, you store it. A floppy disk is storage media. It stores files. To open the file that you stored on the floppy disk, you must put the floppy disk into the floppy disk drive. The floppy disk drive is a storage device in your computer.

Steps

To Use a Floppy Disk

1. Look at the floppy disk. It does not bend. It is hard. It has shiny metal on one end. It has a label on the other end. The disk has two sides, one side has a metal circle.

The computer you use may not have a floppy disk drive.

2. Hold the floppy disk by the label end. Hold the label end with the label up. The metal circle should be facing the floor. The floppy disk drive has a slot.

3. Place the metal end of the floppy disk into the floppy disk drive slot. Push the floppy disk into the drive until you hear a click. The disk is in the drive.

Floppy disks store files.

4. A button is next to the floppy disk drive. Push the button. The disk should pop out a little bit. Use your fingers to pull the disk out of the drive.

Saving a File

You save a file so you can use it again. You save a file on storage media. A floppy disk is storage media that you can take with you. A hard disk is a storage device that is inside the system unit of your computer. The hard disk stores software that you run on your computer. You can save your files on the hard disk, too. In this lesson, you will save a file to the hard disk.

Steps

To Save a File

1. Double-click the File for Burton file icon on the desktop. The File for Burton file opens.

2. Click the Save button on the toolbar. You saved the file!

After you save a file, you can open it again and again.

Computer Safety and Rules

Ethics are rules to help you know whether something is right or wrong. There are rules everyone must follow when using computers. Some rules protect computers so they do not get broken. Some rules protect you so you do not get hurt. Some rules protect others so they do not get hurt.

Protect Computers

A computer costs a lot of money. You must take care of a computer so it does not get broken. You cannot eat or drink while you work on a computer. Do not eat or drink near the computer. Food or even water can harm a computer. Be sure your hands are clean before you type on a keyboard. Hold floppy disks and CD-ROMs properly.

If you have any problems with a computer, ask your teacher or the person who is in charge for help. Do not put heavy objects on the computer. Do not bang or hit the hardware.

Protect You

Make sure an adult knows when you are working on a computer. If you see something on the screen that scares you or makes you sad, tell your teacher.

Protect Information

You always should be considerate of others' work. You should get permission to use things that are not yours. You never should copy somebody's work or software without asking for permission. A copyright means the person who created the work also owns the work.

Protect Privacy

Any information about you, your family, and your friends is personal. Do not give out names, addresses, or telephone numbers to anyone unless you have permission from a member of your family or teacher.

Apply Your Knowledge

Knowing the Parts of the Computer

Now you practice what you have learned so far. You can name the parts of a computer.

Steps

To Name the Parts of the Computer

1. Your teacher will give you a worksheet with a picture of a computer.

2. Draw a circle around the printer.

3. Draw an X over the system unit.

4. Draw a square over the monitor.

5. Write your name over the keyboard.

6. Write a big M on the mouse.

7. Write a big C on the CD-ROM drive.

8. Write a big F on the floppy disk.

You know all the parts of the computer!

Chapter 2

Getting Started with Keyboarding

Keyboarding is using a keyboard to type letters, numbers, and symbols. The keyboard is an input device that is attached to a computer. You use the keyboard to input data into the computer. To type, you press the keys on the keyboard.

What You Will Learn

In this chapter, you will learn how to sit properly at a keyboard. You also will learn the home row keys, the SPACEBAR, the ENTER/RETURN key, and the BACKSPACE key.

Are You Ready to Keyboard?

Keyboarding is using a keyboard to type letters, numbers, and symbols. The keyboard is an input device. You use the keyboard to input data into the computer. To type, you press keys on the keyboard. The letter keys are in rows, but are not in ABC order. The top row on the keyboard has number and symbol keys. Three rows of letter keys are on the keyboard. The keys on the middle row where your fingers rest are called the **home row keys**. Your fingers reach from the home row to other keys on the other rows. The SPACEBAR is the long bar at the bottom of the keyboard.

How you sit at the computer is called **posture**. Practice good posture when you use the keyboard. In this lesson, you will sit using good posture and place your hands correctly on the keyboard.

To Get Ready to Keyboard

1. Sit up straight in your chair, and keep your feet down towards the floor.

2. Curve your fingers slightly and place them on the keyboard.

3. The fingertips on your left hand rest on A, S, D, and F.

Look at the screen. Do not look at the keys. Your hands will learn to find the keys.

4. The fingertips on your right hand rest on J, K, L, and ;.

5. Place your thumbs on _____.

Using the SPACEBAR

The blinking line on the screen is the **insertion point**. The letter, number, or symbol is placed at the insertion point when you press the key on the keyboard. In this lesson, you will learn how to press the SPACEBAR to put spaces between each letter that you type.

The SPACEBAR [＿＿＿＿＿＿] is the long bar at the bottom of the keyboard. Use your right or left thumb to press the SPACEBAR.

To Use the SPACEBAR

1. Place your fingers on the home row keys. Press [A], and then press [_____] with your thumb. The insertion point moved one space to the right.

2. Press [S], press [_____], press [D], press [_____], press [F] and then press [_____].

Remember to use your fingertips to press the letter keys.

3. Press [J], press [_____].

Press [K], press [_____], press [L], press [_____], and then press [:].

Typing the Letter G

In this lesson, you will learn to type the letter g. The G is in the middle row. It is between the home row keys, next to the F. You will use your left pointer finger to press G.

To Type the Letter G

Steps

1. Place your fingers on the home row keys. Lift up your left pointer finger from F and press G.

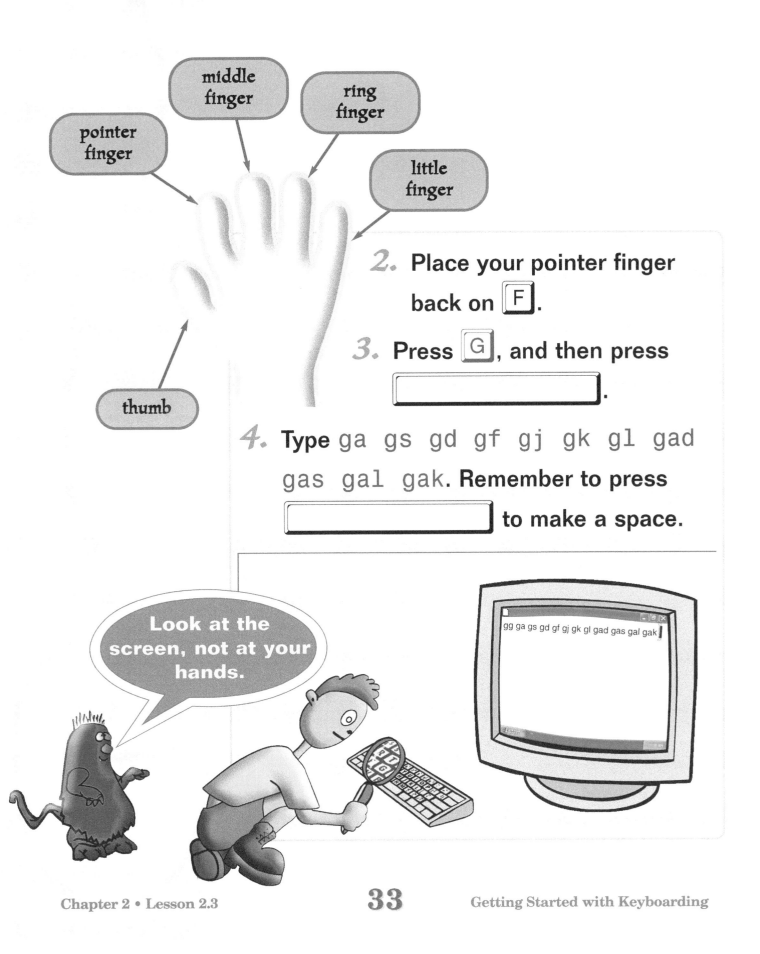

pointer finger

middle finger

ring finger

little finger

thumb

2. Place your pointer finger back on F.

3. Press G, and then press ▢.

4. Type ga gs gd gf gj gk gl gad gas gal gak. Remember to press ▢ to make a space.

Look at the screen, not at your hands.

gg ga gs gd gf gj gk gl gad gas gal gak

Typing the Letter H

In this lesson, you will learn to type the letter h. The H key is in the middle row. It is between the home row keys, next to ⃞J . You will use your right pointer finger to press ⃞H .

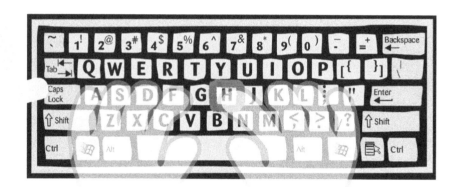

To Type the Letter H

1. Place your fingers on the home row keys. Lift up your right pointer finger from ⃞J and press ⃞H .

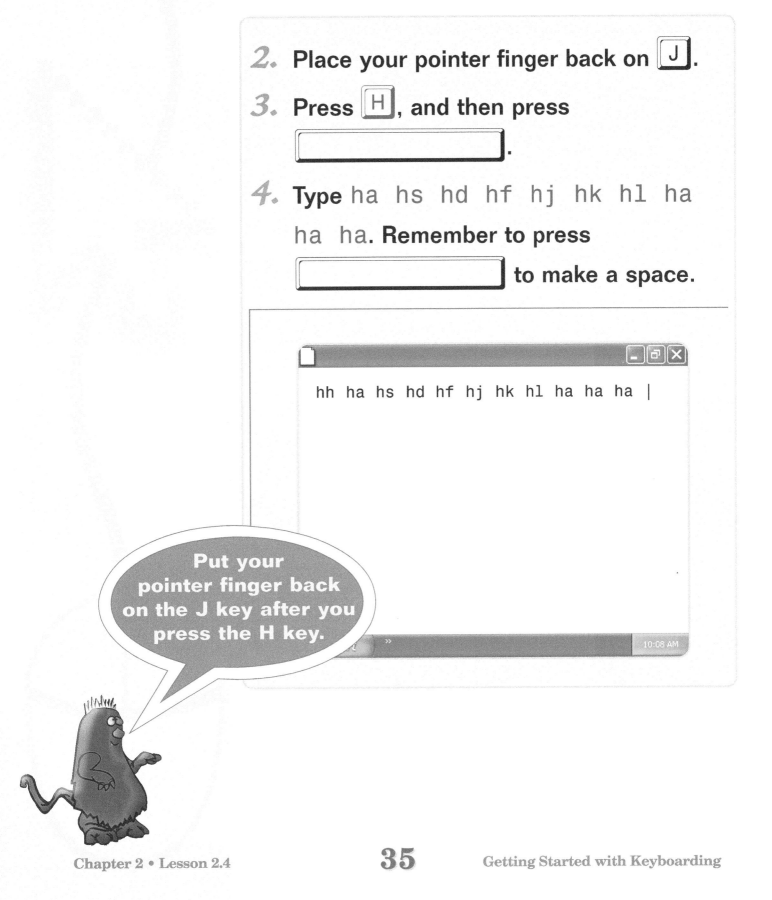

2. Place your pointer finger back on [J].

3. Press [H], and then press [   ].

4. Type ha hs hd hf hj hk hl ha ha ha. Remember to press [   ] to make a space.

hh ha hs hd hf hj hk hl ha ha ha |

Put your pointer finger back on the J key after you press the H key.

Using the ENTER/RETURN Key

The ENTER key is a special key. On some keyboards, it is called the RETURN key. When you press ⌨Enter or ⌨Return, a letter, number, or symbol does not appear on the screen. You sometimes can press ⌨Enter or ⌨Return to give the computer a command. When you type, you can press ⌨Enter or ⌨Return to move the insertion point to the next line. In this lesson, you will learn to use ⌨Enter or ⌨Return.

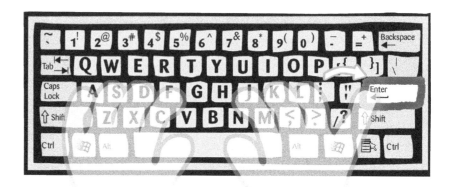

To Use the ENTER/RETURN Key

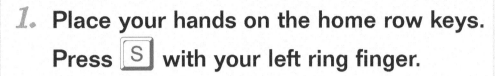

1. Place your hands on the home row keys. Press ⟨S⟩ with your left ring finger.

2. Press ⟨Enter⟩ or ⟨Return⟩. The insertion point moved down to the next line.

3. Type lad lad and then press ⟨Enter⟩ or ⟨Return⟩.

4. Type dad dad and then press ⟨Enter⟩ or ⟨Return⟩.

5. Type gad gad and then press ⟨Enter⟩ or ⟨Return⟩.

```
s
lad lad
dad dad
gad gad
|
```

Using the BACKSPACE Key

The BACKSPACE key is another special key. It works like an eraser. Each time you press ⬅Backspace you erase, or delete, one letter, number, or symbol. You delete whatever is to the left of the insertion point. In this lesson, you will learn to use ⬅Backspace.

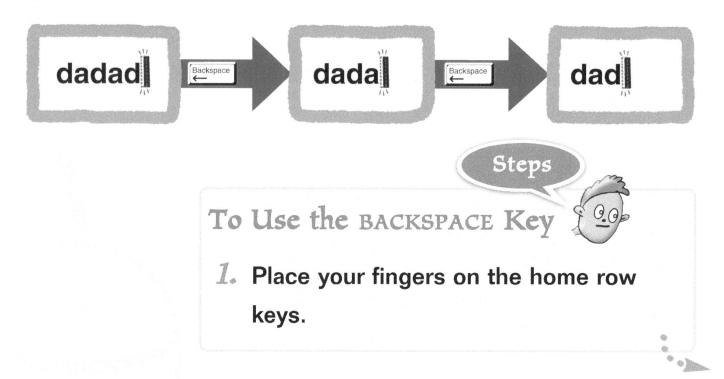

Steps

To Use the BACKSPACE Key

1. Place your fingers on the home row keys.

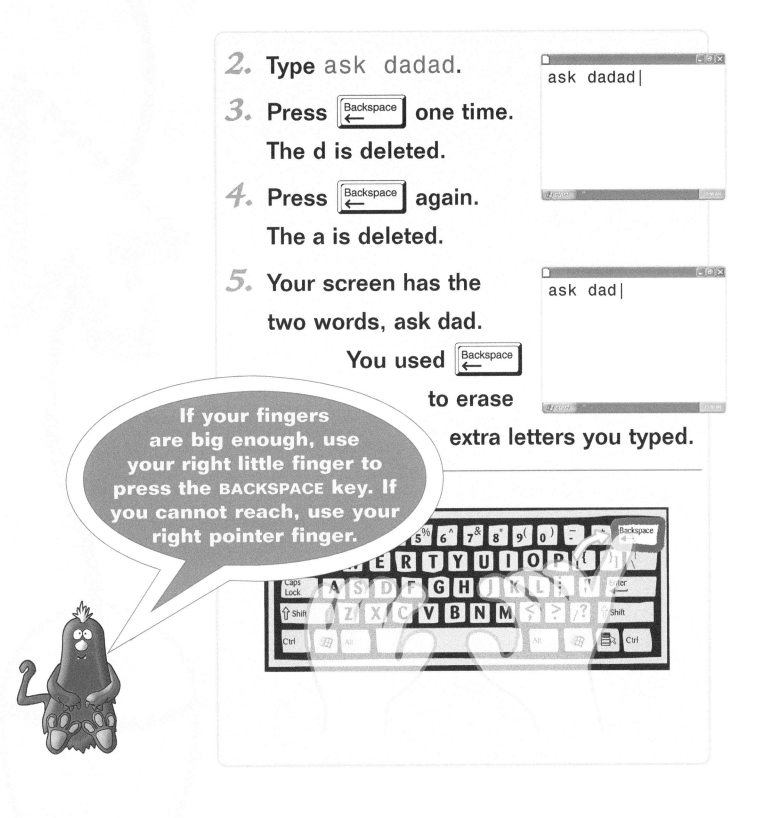

2. Type ask dadad.

3. Press [Backspace←] one time. The d is deleted.

4. Press [Backspace←] again. The a is deleted.

5. Your screen has the two words, ask dad. You used [Backspace←] to erase extra letters you typed.

ask dadad|

ask dad|

> If your fingers are big enough, use your right little finger to press the BACKSPACE key. If you cannot reach, use your right pointer finger.

Typing Words

It takes practice to use the keyboard to type words without looking at your hands. In this lesson, you will begin to type words using the keys that you have learned.

Steps

To Type Words

1. Place your fingers on the home row keys.

2. Type `lad fad sad dad`. **Remember to press** [   ] **to make the space after each word.**

3. **Press** [   ] **two times.**

4. **Type** `lass add` **and then press** [   ] **two times.**

5. **Type** `all dad add`.

You can type words!

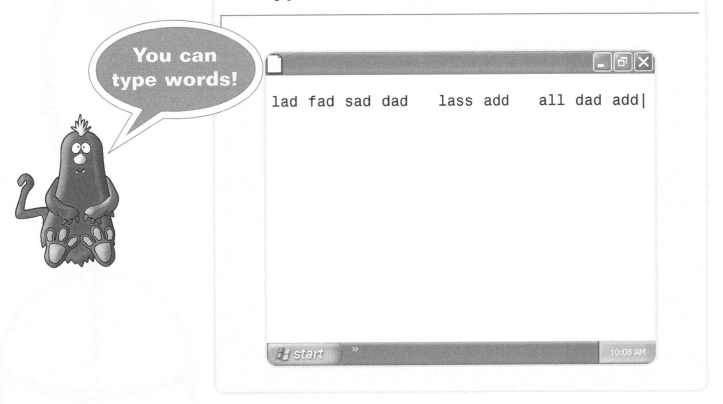

```
lad fad sad dad   lass add   all dad add|
```

Apply Your Knowledge

Keyboarding

Learning to type takes lots of practice. Can you type your name? Can you type simple words?

Steps

To Type Simple Words and Your Name

1. Put your fingers on the home row keys.

2. Type dad gad sad lass lad had.

3. Press [Enter ←] or [Return ←] two times.

4. Type your name.

It is OK to take your fingers off the home row keys to reach all the letters to type your name.

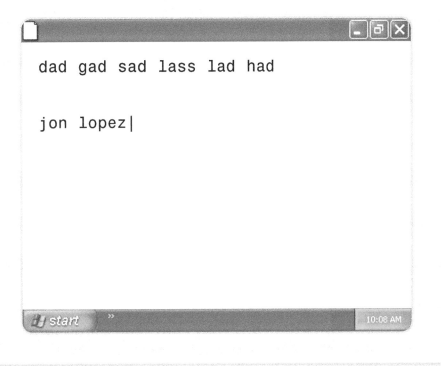

```
dad gad sad lass lad had


jon lopez|
```

Chapter 3

Creating Documents with a Word Processor

A **word processor** is a program on a computer that you use to create documents. A **document** is anything you write using a word processor. Some documents also contain pictures. You can save a document as a file.

Spelling Words

1. pat
2. sat
3. cat
4. mat
5. rat
6. hat
7. bat
8. dog
9. frog
10. log

You are Invited!

Please come to our classroom Thursday at 8:30 a.m. for tea and to see all of our art work. We hope you can come!

Mrs. Brown's 1st Grade Class

What You Will Learn

In this chapter, you will learn how to use a word processor to type letters and numbers, and how to make changes to your work in a document.

What Is Word Processing?

A **word processor** is a computer program you can use to help you write. Word processors save your work in a file called a **document**. A document is what you typed. It can be a story or a poem or homework. You can fix mistakes, move letters, or add words easily. When you make changes, it is called **editing** a document. You can change the shapes and colors of the letters. You can add pictures.

45

Starting the Word Processor

You have to start a word processor before you can use it. You can start the word processor in a few different ways. One way you can start it is by double-clicking the word processor icon on the desktop. The word processor icon is a small little picture; it may look like a little page or a W.

Steps

To Start the Word Processor

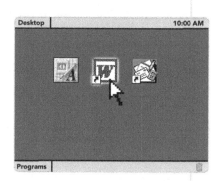

1. Find the word processor icon on your desktop.

2. Double-click the word processor icon.

You see a blank document on the screen. You started the word processor.

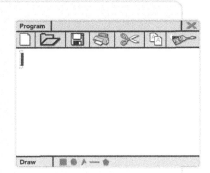

3. Do you see the blinking insertion point? It is near the top of the screen. The insertion point shows you where the next letter, number, or symbol that you type will be placed in the document.

When you type, you create a document.

Typing Capital Letters

Words have two kinds of letters, uppercase and lowercase. The letters on the keyboard keys are uppercase letters. These also are called capital letters. Lowercase letters are smaller. The keyboard has two SHIFT keys. Both SHIFT keys work the same way. You hold down Shift and then you press a letter key to type a capital letter. In this lesson, you will type capital and lowercase letters in a blank document.

48

Creating Documents
with a Word Processor

To Use the SHIFT Key

1. Place your fingers on the home row keys. Press A. You typed a lowercase a.

2. Lift your right little finger off ⠇ and use it to hold down Shift that is next to ?/. Nothing happens when you press Shift without pressing another key at the same time.

3. Press A. You typed a capital A.

4. Stop pressing Shift and type the lowercase letters jkl.

5. Lift your left little finger off A and use it to hold down Shift that is next to Z.

6. Type the capital letters JKL. Now, you can stop pressing Shift.

Your name begins with a capital letter. In the name Burton, the letter B is capital.

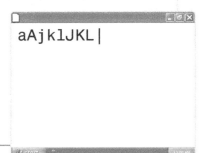

aAjklJKL|

Using the CAPS LOCK Key

The keys on the keyboard do not all work the same. Some keys are called toggle keys. Toggle means you press it to turn it on. A light on the keyboard tells you the key is on. The key stays on until you press it again to turn it off. One toggle key is [Caps Lock]. When you press it to turn it on, all letters you type will be capital letters. In this lesson, you will use [Caps Lock] to type capital letters.

Dd

Aa Bb Cc Ee

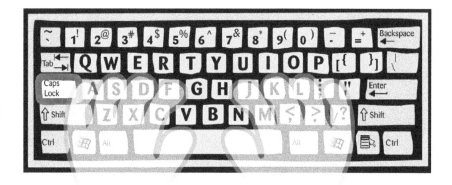

50

Creating Documents
with a Word Processor

To Use the CAPS LOCK Key

CAPS LOCK light

1. Place your fingers on the home row keys.

2. Lift your left little finger off A and use it to press Caps Lock. A light on the keyboard should turn on. This means Caps Lock is on. Put your little finger back on A.

3. Type DAD DAD LAD LAD.

4. Press Caps Lock. The light on the keyboard should turn off. This means Caps Lock is off.

5. Type dad dad lad lad.

DAD DAD LAD LAD dad dad lad lad|

51

Creating Documents
with a Word Processor

Typing Numbers and Symbols

You used Shift to type capital letters. You also use Shift to type symbols. Some symbols are on top of the numbers on the number keys. You have to hold down Shift and then press the number key to type the symbol on that key. Some symbols are on keys on the bottom row. You will use Shift to type symbols.

52

To Use the SHIFT Key

1. Hold down [Shift] that is next to [?/] with your right little finger.

2. Keep holding down [Shift], reach up with your left little finger, and press [!/1] that is on the top row. You typed the exclamation point symbol!

If your fingers are too small to reach the top row when your hands are on the home row keys, you can lift your hand and use your pointer finger.

3. Hold down [Shift] that is next to [?/], reach up with your left ring finger, and then press [@/2] on the top row. You typed the @ symbol. It is called the at symbol.

4. Do not press `Shift`. Use your pointer finger to type the numbers 1234567890. If you do not press `Shift`, you type numbers.

!@1234567890|

Editing Your Work

Letters, numbers, and symbols are called **characters**. The BACKSPACE key deletes the character you just typed. Each time you press ⌫Backspace you delete one character. You can use ⌫Backspace to edit your document. When you **edit**, you change your work to make it better. In this lesson, you will use ⌫Backspace to delete letters you typed.

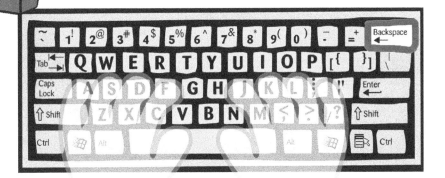

To Use the BACKSPACE Key to Edit

1. Place your fingers on the home row keys.

2. Type A sad.

   A sad|

3. Press **Backspace ←** with your right little finger three times. The d, the a, and the s are deleted from your screen.

   You edited your work to make it better!

4. Type glad lad.

   A glad lad|

Using the ENTER/RETURN Key

When you type in a word processor program, you can fill up a line with letters and words. If no more room is on the line, the insertion point moves down to the next line. This is called word wrap. When you type, you can press ⌨Enter or ⌨Return to force the insertion point to move down to the next line. In this lesson, you will use ⌨Enter or ⌨Return to force a new line.

Press the ENTER/RETURN key with your right little finger.

57

To Use the ENTER/RETURN Key

1. Place your hands on the home row keys. Press ⌨S with your left ring finger. Keep pressing ⌨S until the line is full. When the insertion point reaches the end of the line, the next s you type will word wrap to the next line.

> **Remember to turn the CAPS LOCK key off to type lowercase letters.**

2. Press 〔Enter ←〕 or 〔Return ←〕. The insertion point moves to a new line.

3. Type `lad  lad` and then press 〔Enter ←〕 or 〔Return ←〕.

4. Type `dad  dad` and then press 〔Enter ←〕 or 〔Return ←〕.

5. Type `gad  gad` and then press 〔Enter ←〕 or 〔Return ←〕.

word wrap

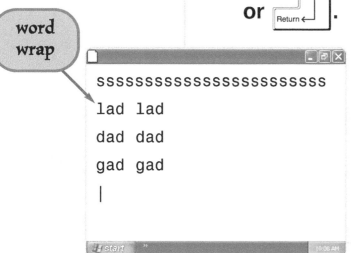

```
sssssssssssssssssssssssss
lad lad
dad dad
gad gad
|
```

Apply Your Knowledge

Word Processing

In this activity, you will use the skills you learned in this chapter to type your name and your age. You also will type a symbol.

Steps

To Type Your Name and Age

1. Double-click the word processor icon on your desktop. The blank document is ready for you to type.

2. Hold down ⌈Shift⌋, then type the first letter of your first name.

3. Stop pressing ⌈Shift⌋ and type the rest of the letters in your first name. Press ⌈   ⌋.

4. Type your last name. Be sure to start it with a capital letter. Press **Enter ←** or **Return ←** to move the insertion point down to the next line.

5. Type your age on the new line. Press **Enter ←** or **Return ←** to move down to the next line.

6. Hold down **Shift**, and press **★8** to type a row of * on the new line. Use word wrap to fill the first line and start a new line.

You are a star!

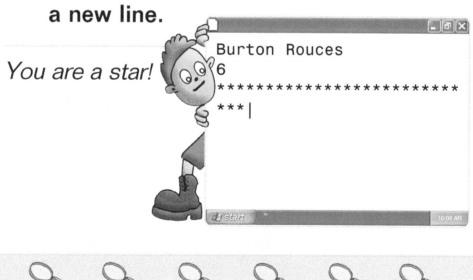

```
Burton Rouces
6
*************************
***
```

Chapter 4

Networks and the Internet

A computer can work alone. Computers also can be connected to each other. You can share files and communicate using computers on a **network**. The Internet is a huge network that connects computers all over the world. These connected computers can communicate with each other.

What You Will Learn

In this chapter, you will learn about networks. You also will use the Internet to look at Web pages on the World Wide Web.

What Are the Internet and the Web?

The Internet is thousands of networks that connect millions of computers all over the world. The World Wide Web — also called the Web — is part of the Internet. The Web has millions of Web pages. Web pages have lessons, news, pictures, stories, and music. You can learn about the world by looking at Web pages. You can use the Internet if you work on a computer that is connected to the Internet.

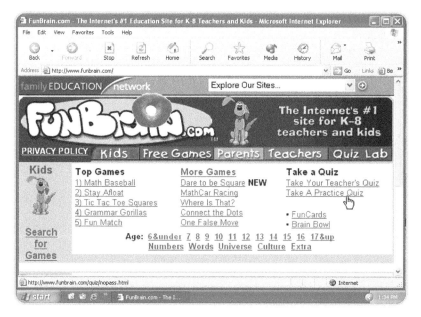

Looking at Web Pages

A Web page is a document on the World Wide Web. A browser is a program that lets you look at Web pages on a computer. You click links on Web pages to look at other Web pages. Some links are words, and some links are pictures. Each Web page has an address so you can find it on the Web. The address is at the top of the browser on your screen. A home page is the first Web page you see when you visit a Web site. A Web site is a group of Web pages. Web pages can be quite big. Some Web pages are too big to fit on the screen at one time. To see the rest of the page, you need to scroll. Scroll means you move through the page on the screen so you can see a different part of the document or Web page. You click the scroll box to scroll a document.

burtonsclass.com

To Look at a Web Page

1. **Double-click the icon on the desktop to start the browser on your computer.**

2. **Look at the home page. Do you see pictures? Do you see words? Do you hear sounds?**

3. **Do you see the scroll box on the side of the window? If so, click in the lower part of the scroll box. Do you see more of the Web page?**

Each Web page has an address so you can find it on the Internet.

scroll box

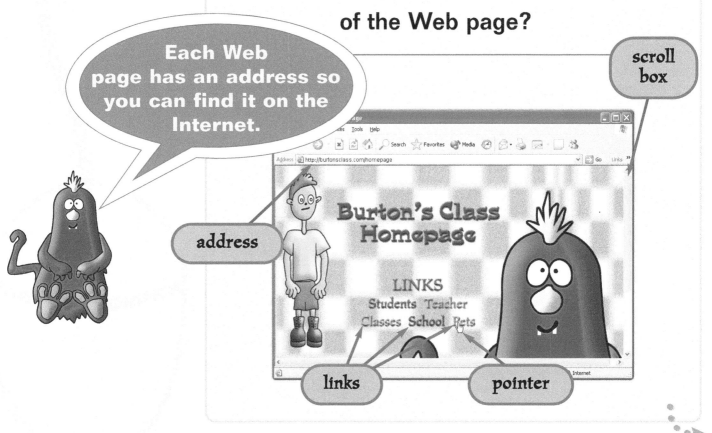

address

links

pointer

4. Move the mouse pointer. Does the pointer change shape? When your pointer changes shape and looks like a hand, you are on a link. When you click a link on a Web page, you will view another Web page.

5. Click a link. A new Web page is on the screen. It has a new address. The picture on this page in this book shows you a Web page in a browser. If you click the **Back button**, you will go back to the page you just saw. The Back button is on the top row of buttons on your screen.

6. Click the Back button. The home page should be on your screen.

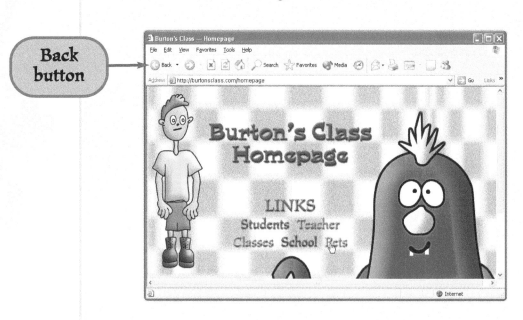

Back button

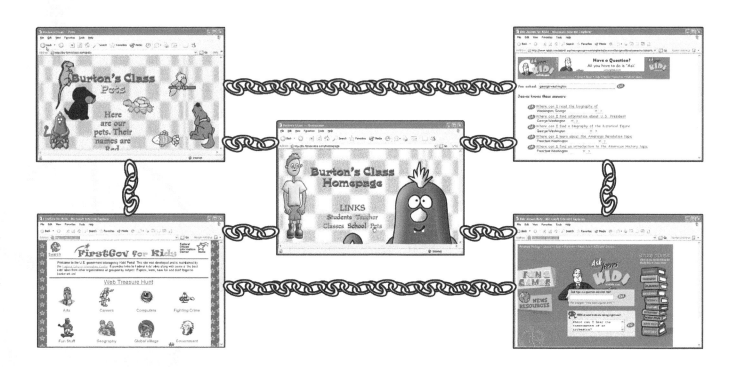

Safety on the Internet

The Web can be a fun place to visit. Many good things are on the Internet. Some bad things also are on the Internet. Just like you have to be safe at school and home, you have to be safe on the Internet.

Rules w ill help you stay safe. Your school has an acceptable use policy (AUP). An acceptable use policy is a set of rules for everyone to follow when using computers and the Internet. Your teacher will help you learn all these rules.

Visiting Web pages is fun.

If you see a page that has strange pictures or words, click the Close button and go find your teacher or the person in charge.

Here are five simple rules to follow while you are on the Internet.

1. Always tell your teacher when you go on the Internet.

2. Be polite when you are on the Internet.

3. If you see a Web page that makes you feel scared or sad, quit the program and go find the person in charge.

4. E-mail is a way to send a message to someone through the Internet. Be sure you know who sent you the e-mail before you open the message.

5. Never use e-mail to send bad words or say mean things to other people on the Internet.

Have a nice day!

Apply Your Knowledge

Looking at Web Pages

In this activity, you will use what you have learned in this chapter to look at a Web page.

Steps

To Look at a Web Page

1. Ask your teacher to type this Web page address in the browser www.yahooligans.com to go to the Yahooligans Web page. This Web site has pictures, videos, and stories. The home page has links to many other Web pages.

2. Scroll to see the whole page.

3. Move the pointer on the page until you see the hand pointer. Click the link.

4. You see a new Web page. Click the Back button.

5. Click a link that is a word.

6. Click a link that is a picture.

You can play games and learn about science, history, math, and much more by visiting Web pages.

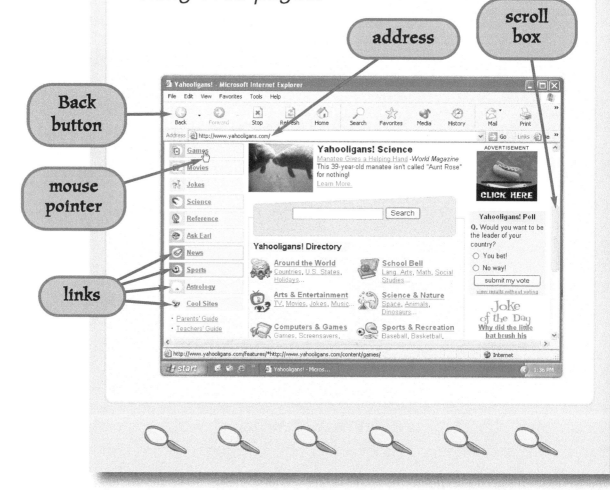

Chapter 5

Creating Graphics

When you visit a Web page on the Internet, you might see that it contains different kinds of graphics. Graphics are pictures, videos, or photographs. Computer graphics also can be printed as posters, in magazines, and in books. You can use a paint or draw program to create pictures for your friends, family, or teachers.

What You Will Learn

In this chapter, you will learn how to use paint and drawing tools to create colorful shapes and pictures.

Lesson 5.1

What Are Paint and Draw Tools?

When you want to create your own pictures, shapes, or lines using the computer, you can use a paint or drawing program. Every drawing program has drawing tools in a toolbox. A toolbox is a row of buttons or icons. These tools help you paint and draw using the computer. You use the mouse to control the tools. You point, click, double-click, and drag the mouse to tell the computer where and how to draw. White space, or canvas, is the blank area on the screen that you use to create graphics.

Eraser tool

Pencil tool

Airbrush tool

Line tool

Rectangle tool

Ellipse tool

Fill With Color tool

Brush tool

Text tool

canvas

color box

untitled -

File   Edit   View

For Help, click Help Topics on the Help Men

Using the Brush Tool

In this lesson, you will start the Paint or Draw program on your computer and use the Brush tool, also called the Paint Brush tool. The Brush tool draws thick lines. The icon for the brush tool looks like a paint brush.

Steps

To Use the Brush Tool

1. Start the Paint or Draw program on your computer. Point to the Brush tool in the toolbox.

2. Click the Brush tool.

tool options

3. Point to the canvas. The pointer has a new shape when you move it onto the canvas. It looks like this: ╌┼╌

4. Point near the top of the canvas. Hold down the left mouse button and then drag the Brush tool pointer down to draw a line.

5. Release the left mouse button to stop drawing.

6. Drag the Brush tool pointer to draw two more lines so you have three lines.

The Brush tool draws lines like a paintbrush would paint.

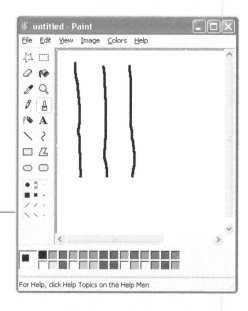

Using Tool Options

Options mean choices. Tool options allow you to choose shapes and sizes for some of the paint and draw tools. You get to pick the width of the brush line when you use the Brush tool. Tool options are below the paint and draw toolbox when you click a tool that has options.

Steps

To Use Tool Options

1. Click the Brush tool in the toolbox.

2. Tool options are displayed below the toolbox.

3. Click a wide brush shape in the toolbox. The pointer changes to look like this: It will draw a wider line.

4. Drag the Brush tool pointer in the canvas to draw a thick line.

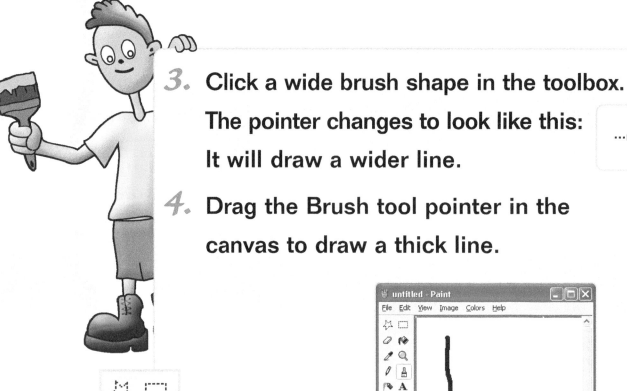

Brush tool

wide brush

narrow brush

tool options

Using the Color Box

The color box contains 28 different colors. In this lesson, you will select and use seven colors from the color box to make a rainbow of colors: red, orange, , green, blue, indigo, and violet.

Start with a new, clean canvas. Click File on the menu bar, click New, then click No (you do not want to save your work just yet).

Steps

To Use the Color Box

1. Click the Brush tool in the toolbox.

2. Click the color red in the color box. You see the box turn red, and your brush will draw red.

The color of your brush!

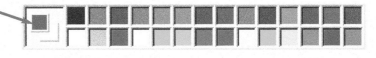

3. Click the canvas and then drag the Brush tool pointer to draw the red arch in the rainbow.

4. Click the color orange in the color box and then drag the Brush tool pointer to draw the orange arch below the red one.

5. Draw the remaining colors of the rainbow in this order: yellow, green, blue, indigo, and violet.

Creating Shapes

Shape tools, let you create all kinds of different shapes. The **Rectangle tool** draws a shape with four sides. The **Ellipse** tool draws a round shape. You can use Shift to create squares and circles. In this lesson, you will create three shapes.

Start with a new, clean canvas. At the top of the program, click File, click New, and then click No (you do not want to save your work just yet).

Steps

To Create Perfect Shapes

1. Click the Rectangle tool in the toolbox.

2. Hold down Shift.

3. While you still are holding down Shift, point to the top of the canvas where you want the shape to begin. The pointer looks like this:

4. Drag the Rectangle pointer down and away from the starting point on the canvas. Release Shift. You drew a square.

> **All four sides are the same size in a square.**

5. Click the Ellipse tool. Hold down Shift and then point to where you want the middle of the circle.

6. Drag the Ellipse pointer to draw a round shape, then release Shift. You drew a circle.

7. The Rounded Rectangle tool draws a shape with four sides that has rounded corners.

8. Click the Rounded Rectangle tool. Point to the canvas where you want the shape to begin.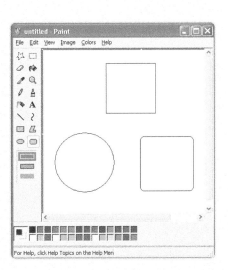

9. Hold down Shift and then drag the mouse pointer to draw a square with rounded corners.

The more you drag, the bigger the shape!

Using the Fill With Color Tool

The **Fill With Color tool** fills the inside of a shape with color. In this lesson, you will fill shapes with different colors using the Fill With Color tool, also called the Paint Can or Paint Bucket tool.

Start with a new, clean canvas. Click File, click New, and then click No.

Steps

To Use the Fill With Color Tool

1. Use the Rectangle, Ellipse, and Rounded Rectangle tools to draw three different shapes on the canvas.

2. Click the Fill With Color tool in the toolbox.

3. Click your favorite color in the color box.

4. Click inside one of the shapes. The shape fills with the color you picked from the color box.

5. Click inside each shape to fill each with a different color using the Fill With Color tool.

Using the Eraser Tool

The Eraser tool works like an eraser. The pointer will have a special shape when you are using the eraser. You can use tool options to make the eraser bigger or smaller. Drag the Eraser tool pointer over lines or colors on the canvas to make that area white again. The Eraser tool helps you edit your drawing. In this lesson, you will use the Eraser tool to erase part of a picture.

Start with a new, clean canvas. Click File, click New, and then click No.

To Use the Eraser Tool

Steps

1. Use the Ellipse and Brush tools to draw a face. Draw the eyes, a nose, a mouth, ears, and hair.

2. Click the Eraser tool in the toolbox. Click the smallest eraser size in the toolbox.

3. Point to the right eye on the face you just drew. Drag the mouse a little bit. As you drag the Eraser pointer over the eye, it is erased.

4. Drag the Eraser tool pointer back and forth to rub out the eye on the face.

5. Click the Ellipse or Brush tool to draw the eye again.

Using the Airbrush Tool

The Airbrush tool sprays color. It might remind you of using a can of spray paint. If you leave the airbrush in one place and continue to hold down the mouse button, the area will fill with color. In this lesson, you will use the Airbrush tool to spray a picture.

Start with a new, clean canvas. Click File, click New, and then click No.

To Use the Airbrush Tool

Steps

1. Click the Airbrush tool in the toolbox.

2. Click a spray size in the toolbox and then click brown in the color box.

3. Place the Airbrush pointer on the canvas. Notice the shape of the pointer.

4. Click the mouse to spray a dot. Drag the Airbrush pointer to draw a little line.

5. Use the Airbrush pointer to draw a tree that has a brown trunk and green leaves.

Using the Line Tool

The Line tool draws straight lines. You can make lines different widths and different colors. In this lesson, you will use the Line tool to create a line drawing of a tic-tac-toe board.

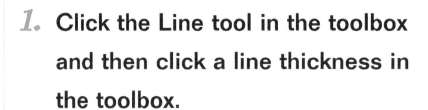

To Use the Line Tool

1. Click the Line tool in the toolbox and then click a line thickness in the toolbox.

2. Move the Line pointer onto the canvas. The pointer looks like this: You will draw a tic-tac-toe board.

3. Point to the area on the canvas where you want the first line to begin.

4. Drag the mouse pointer down to draw a straight line. Stop dragging, move the mouse pointer to a new place on the canvas, then draw another line.

5. Draw a tic-tac-toe board and then draw the first X.

Use the Ellipse tool to draw a circle and play tic-tac-toe with your friend!

Using the Pencil Tool

The Pencil tool lets you draw using the mouse. You can write words or do simple line drawings in different colors using the Pencil tool. In this lesson, you will write your name using the Pencil tool.

Steps

To Use the Pencil Tool

1. Click the Pencil tool in the toolbox.

2. Click a color in the color box.

3. Move the pointer onto the canvas. The mouse pointer looks like a pencil.

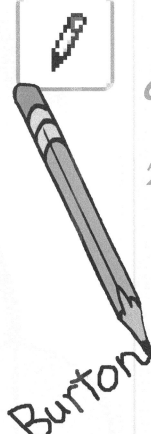

4. Click the pencil pointer on the canvas where you want the first line to begin and then drag to write the first letter of your first name.

5. Stop dragging. Move the mouse pointer and then drag to draw the next letter.

6. Finish writing your first name using the Pencil tool.

7. Use the Eraser tool to erase any mistakes you might make and then try again.

Using the Text Tool

The Text tool is used to type words to describe your pictures. In this lesson, you draw a picture and then type a word describing the picture.

Burton

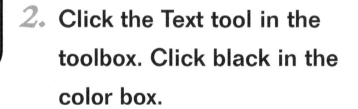

Steps

To Use the Text Tool

1. Draw a colorful picture using your favorite paint and draw tools. Leave space at the bottom.

2. Click the Text tool in the toolbox. Click black in the color box.

3. Point to the white space near the bottom on the left side of your picture.

4. Drag the Text tool pointer to create a small box.

When you create a box, you will see a new toolbar open on your screen. This is a Fonts toolbar. You can use it to change the way the letters you type will look.

5. Use the keyboard to type a word or two in the box.

6. After you type, click outside the box. The box is gone, but the words you typed appear in your drawing.

7. Ask your teacher to help you print your drawing.

My Rabbit Tasha

Apply Your Knowledge

Drawing with the Paint and Draw Tools

In this activity, you will use the different paint and draw tools that you have learned about to draw a picture for your teacher. Be sure to use different colors in the color box. Use the Eraser tool if you make mistakes. Once you are done drawing a picture, you will type your name.

Steps

To Draw Using the Paint and Draw Tools

1. Use your favorite paint and draw tools to draw a picture for your teacher.

2. Click the Text tool and then click your favorite color in the color box.

3. Drag the Text tool to create a box.

4. Use the keyboard to type your name in the box.

5. Ask your teacher to help you print your drawing.

6. Quit the drawing program.

Miguel

Chapter 6

Working with Presentation Software

Presentation software is used to make presentations. Computer presentations are called slide shows. Slide shows can teach, train you to do a task, or be just for fun. Slides can include words, pictures, video, photographs, and sounds.

What You Will Learn

In this chapter, you will learn about presentation software, the definitions of the words used to create presentations, and how to create and watch a slide show.

What Is Multimedia?

Media can be paint, ink, paper, pictures, photographs, text, words, or video. Multi means many. If you create multimedia, it means you are using more than one type of media. Computers can display video, words, sounds, and images at one time using presentation software. Multimedia puts more than one type of media together at one time. Presentations are fun to create and watch.

97

Working with
Presentation Software

Presentation Definitions

Presentation software is a program that creates slide shows. You create a slide by putting words, video, clip art, and sounds together. A presentation can have many slides. You can animate pictures or words on a slide. **Animate** means to make it move. You can animate text. Animation is what makes slides fun to watch. Slides can have video. **Video** is any movie. You can put clip art on slides. **Clip art** is a group of pictures that come with the software. Slides can play **sound**, like a recording of your voice, a noise, or a song.

> You would put a very short video on a slide.

98

Creating a Slide

You have to start a presentation program before you can create or look at slides. You can have a slide show on your computer that you can watch. You can start the software in different ways. One way you can start it is by double-clicking the presentation program icon on the desktop. The presentation program icon may look like a little slide or a P.

Steps

To Create a Slide

1. **Start the presentation program on your computer.**

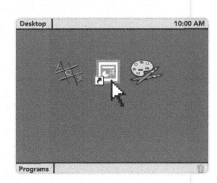

99

Working with
Presentation Software

2. Look at the first slide that opens. Each slide starts out like a blank page. You can put pictures, words, or any type of media on the slide.

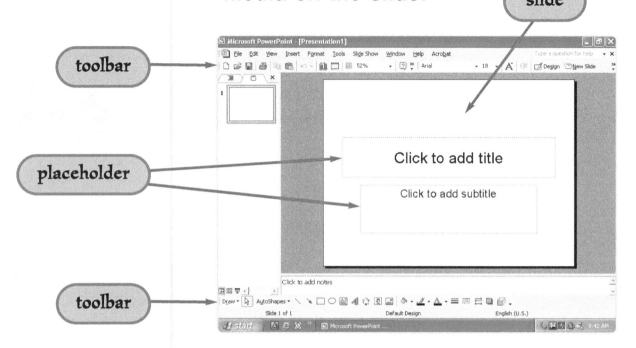

toolbar

slide

placeholder

toolbar

3. The toolbars on your screen have many tools that you can use to create your slides.

4. If the slide has a Click to add title placeholder on your screen, click it and then type your name. You started your presentation.

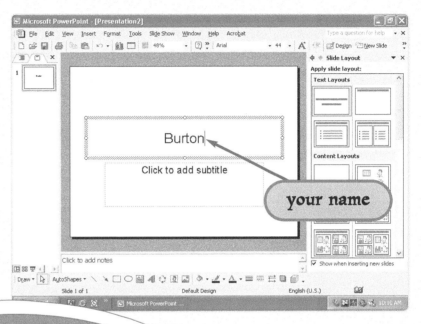

You can add as many slides as you want to a slide show. You can add pictures and animation to make your slide show fun to watch!

Apply Your Knowledge

Watching a Slide Show

You can use a slide show to tell a story, send a message to a friend, or teach a class. You will look at a slide show that was made by a friend. This friend used presentation software to tell a story about his party.

Steps

To Watch a Slide Show

1. **Double-click the MyBirthdayParty presentation icon on your desktop.**

2. The presentation opens.

Slide Show (from current slide) button

slide 1

3. Click the Slide Show (from the current slide) button.

4. Look at the show. You will see a lot of multimedia on the slides.

That was fun!

Chapter 7

Working with Spreadsheets

Spreadsheets are programs that work with numbers. People use spreadsheets at home to keep track of their money. Teachers use spreadsheets to track grades and attendance. Store owners use spreadsheets to figure out how much items should cost.

What You Will Learn

In this chapter, you will learn how spreadsheets are used, the definition of the words that explain spreadsheets, and how to find and enter data in a spreadsheet.

What Is a Spreadsheet?

Spreadsheet software helps people work with numbers using a computer. Spreadsheets help answer number questions. Numbers and words are entered in rows and columns. Words let you know what the numbers mean.

You can use a spreadsheet to find out how many boys and girls in your school like chocolate, vanilla, or mint ice cream.

girls

total

boys

$1 + 4 = 5$ Chocola
$5 + 5 = 10$ Vanilla
$3 + 4 = 7$ Mint

$1 + 4 = 5$
$5 + 5 = 10$
$3 + 4$

Spreadsheet Definitions

A **column** runs up and down the page. A spreadsheet contains many columns. Each column is identified by a letter. The letters are in ABC order. A **row** runs across the page. A spreadsheet has many rows. Rows are in 1, 2, 3 order. A **cell** is each box where a column and row meet. The **active cell** has a dark border around it. When you type, what you type appears in the active cell. You type numbers in cells.

Numbers are called **values**. They tell you how much or how many. You also type words in cells. In a spreadsheet, words are called labels. **Labels** tell you what the numbers mean.

columns

rows

	A	B	C	D	E
1		Boys	Girls	Total	
2	Choc	1	4	5	
3	Van	5	5	10	
4	Mint	3	4	7	
5					
6					
7					
8					

value

label

active cell

dark border

cells

Lesson 7.3

Opening a Spreadsheet

In this lesson, you will open a spreadsheet file that your teacher put on the computer desktop. This file is named Pets. This is a spreadsheet that counts how many students in Mrs. Rice's first grade class have pets. Each type of pet is listed.

To Open a Spreadsheet

Steps

1. **Double-click the Pets spreadsheet icon. The Pets spreadsheet opens in the spreadsheet program. You can see the columns and rows. This file has labels and values.**

Do you have a pet?

	A	B
1	*Pets*	
2	**Type of Pet**	**Number**
3	*birds*	3
4	*cats*	5
5	*dogs*	9
6	*fish*	4
7	*other pets*	2
8	**Total**	23

Moving Around a Spreadsheet

When you type a number or word, it appears in the active cell. You can change which cell is the active cell in a spreadsheet by pressing the ARROW keys on the keyboard. You also can click a cell to make it the active cell. In this lesson, you will learn how to move around a spreadsheet.

Steps

To Move Around a Spreadsheet

1. The cell with the dark border is called the active cell.

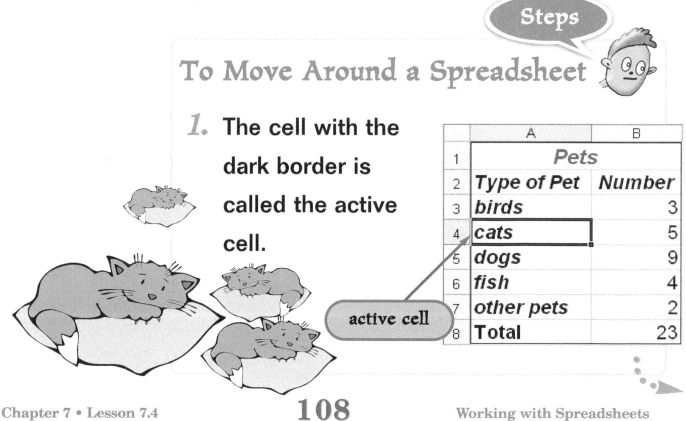

active cell

	A	B
1	Pets	
2	Type of Pet	Number
3	birds	3
4	cats	5
5	dogs	9
6	fish	4
7	other pets	2
8	Total	23

2. Press ⬇ one time. The active cell now is on the next row.

3. Press ➡ one time. The active cell now is in the next column.

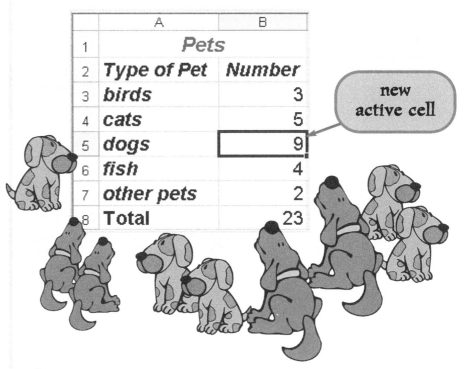

new active cell

4. Point to a cell in the middle of the screen and then click. The active cell now is the cell that you clicked.

Finding the Cell Address

Spreadsheets have many rows and many columns. Each cell in the spreadsheet has its own address. The cell address tells you where the cell is in the spreadsheet. To find the address of the cell, you have to look at the names of the columns and rows. Column names are the letters across the top of the spreadsheet. Row names are the numbers down the left side of the spreadsheet. In this lesson, you will find the address of the active cell.

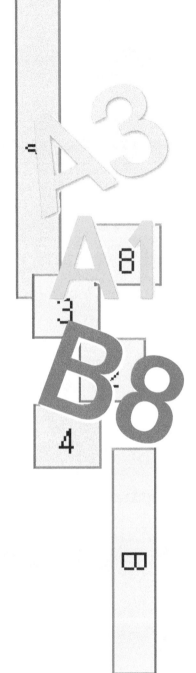

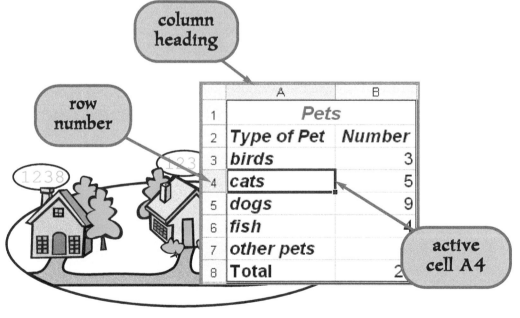

To Find the Cell Address

Steps

1. Find the column that has letter B on the top.

2. Find the row that has number 2 on the side.

3. Use the mouse to click the cell that is in column B and in row 2. The address of this cell is B2. The dark border around cell B2 shows that it is now the active cell. B2 is the address for this active cell.

	A	B
1	*Pets*	
2	**Type of Pet**	**Number**
3	*birds*	3
4	*cats*	5
5	*dogs*	9
6	*fish*	4
7	*other pets*	2
8	**Total**	23

4. Press ⟶. The active cell now is cell C2.

Understanding Spreadsheet Information

The spreadsheet on your screen is used to total the number of different pets for a class of students. In this lesson, you will use the spreadsheet to answer how much and how many questions about this class's pets.

Steps

To Understand Spreadsheet Information

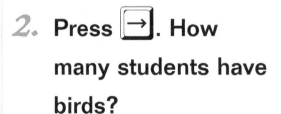

1. Click the cell with birds as the label. This is cell A3.

2. Press →. How many students have birds?

	Pets	
	Type of Pet	**Number**
3	*birds*	3
4	*cats*	5
5	*dogs*	9
6	*fish*	4
7	*other pets*	2
8	Total	23

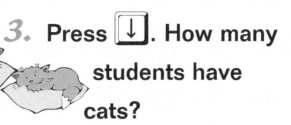

3. Press ⬇. How many students have cats?

4. Press ⬇. How many students have dogs?

5. Click the cell that has the label Total. This is cell A8.

6. Press ➡. There is a formula in cell B8. This formula adds up all the numbers that are in the cells above it.

7. The spreadsheet formula added the numbers 3, 5, 9, 4, and 2, for you. A total of 23 students in the class have pets.

Apply Your Knowledge

Creating Your Class Spreadsheet

Using what you have learned in this chapter, you will help your class create a spreadsheet that shows the different types of pets owned by your classmates.

Steps

To Create the Favorite Pets Class Spreadsheet

1. Double-click the Class Pets spreadsheet icon on your computer desktop. The spreadsheet opens.

2. Ask your class how many students have each animal. Total the numbers.

3. Type the total number for each pet in the Number column (this is column B) next to the name of each animal.

4. Look at the total number. Does it change each time you type in a new number? The formula in cell B8 adds up the numbers.

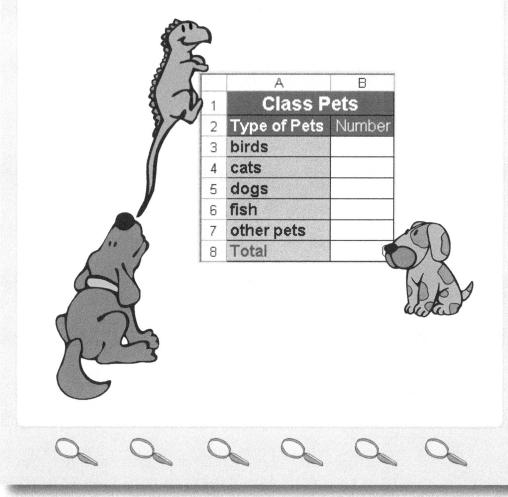

	A	B
1	**Class Pets**	
2	**Type of Pets**	Number
3	birds	
4	cats	
5	dogs	
6	fish	
7	other pets	
8	Total	

Chapter 8

Working with Information in Databases

Databases store data. A database organizes data so you can find information. Many types of databases are used. An address book is a database that stores names, addresses, and phone numbers. A dictionary is a database of words and definitions. An encyclopedia is a database of facts about the world.

Burton's Phone Book

Joseph	555-0987
Janna	555-6385
Weis	555-2158
Susan	555-1253

Encyclopedia

What You Will Learn

In this chapter, you will learn to use databases and some of the words that explain databases. You will learn how to start your own database.

116

What Is a Database?

A database is a collection of data. A database for you might be a list of all your friends. The data in your friend database might include their name, birthday, address, pet, and phone number. Your school uses a database to track all the students in the school. That database is a large one. It stores their names, addresses, phone numbers, parent information, and grades. To create a database on the computer, you use database software.

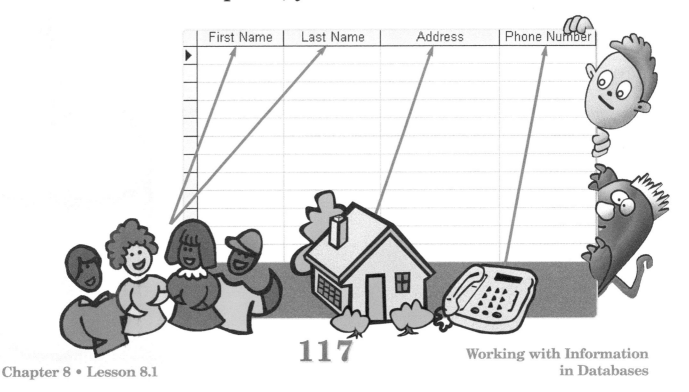

First Name	Last Name	Address	Phone Number

117

Working with Information
in Databases

Database Definitions

A field stores one piece of data. You might have databases with all the students in your class. In this database, each child's first name is in one field, street address is in another field, phone number is in another field, and birthday is in another field.

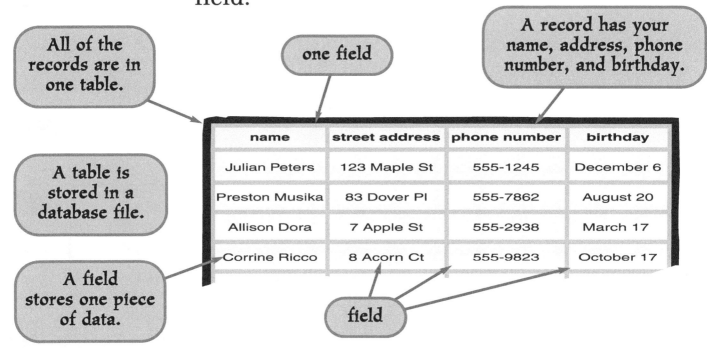

All of the records are in one table.

one field

A record has your name, address, phone number, and birthday.

A table is stored in a database file.

name	street address	phone number	birthday
Julian Peters	123 Maple St	555-1245	December 6
Preston Musika	83 Dover Pl	555-7862	August 20
Allison Dora	7 Apple St	555-2938	March 17
Corrine Ricco	8 Acorn Ct	555-9823	October 17

A field stores one piece of data.

field

Each record is a group of fields that have something in common. If your class had 15 kids, there would be 15 records. Your record has your name, address, phone number, and birthday. All of the records are in one table. The table is stored in a database file.

First Name	Last Name	Phone Number	Address	Pet Name
YOUR NAME	YOUR LAST NAME	555-1232	8 Maple Rd	Leroy

Working with Information
in Databases

Getting Information from the Database

You get information from a database by asking questions. In this lesson, you will learn how you might get information about a class of students. Your teacher will help you answer the questions.

Steps

To Get Information from the Database

1. **Where does Jen live?**

2. **What is Mike's last name?**

3. **What is Hector's phone number?**

4. **What is the name of Emily's dog?**

First Name	Last Name	Phone Number	Address	Pet Name
Jen	Laina	555-1232	8 Maple Rd	Leroy
Mike	Presto	555-8765	23 Main St	Guapo
Hector	Lopez	555-9876	1 First St	Spot
Emily	Christos	555-9862	45 Elm Ave	Fido

Apply Your Knowledge

Creating Your Class Database

You have learned about databases, what they are used for, and some words used with databases. In this activity, you will help your class create a list that can be put into a database on the computer. The database will have the first name and birth dates of each student in your class.

Steps

To Create Your Class Database

1. Create a list on a paper.

2. Draw two columns.

3. Write the first names of five students in your class down one column.

4. Write their birth dates next to their names.

You are helling to create a database!

Name	Birthday
Rebecca	August 10
Zach	February 9
Joanna	April 16
Tanya	May 10
Michael	March 17